Written by Jon Richards • Illustrated by Josy Bloggs

W

First published in Great Britain
in 2020 by The Watts Publishing Group
Copyright © The Watts Publishing Group, 2020
All rights reserved

Series editor: Julia Bird
Produced by Tall Tree Ltd
Editor: Lara Murphy
Designer: Ed Simkins
Artist: Josy Bloggs

HB ISBN: 978 1 4451 6986 6
PB ISBN: 978 1 4451 6987 3

Franklin Watts
An imprint of Hachette Children's Group
Part of The Watts Publishing Group
Carmelite House
50 Victoria Embankment
London EC4Y 0DZ

An Hachette UK Company
www.hachette.co.uk
www.hachettechildrens.co.uk

Printed in China

MIX
Paper from
responsible sources
FSC
www.fsc.org
FSC® C104740

Contents

A world in motion

All around the world, animals are moving from one place to another, making regular journeys called migrations. But why do they make these amazing and often dangerous journeys?

Drinking water
Animals often migrate to find water. Weather patterns change over the course of a year and rains can dry up. When the rains stop, animals move to places where there is more water.

Finding food
A lack of rain also usually brings a lack of food, as plants die quickly without water. Animals have to move to places where plants are still thriving so that they have enough to eat. Warmer weather can often cause a boom in food, attracting animals from far away.

MIGRATION RECORDS

SMALLEST MIGRANT
ZOOPLANKTON
1-2 MM LONG

LARGEST MIGRANT
BLUE WHALE
UP TO 27 M LONG

Animal nursery
A place that is rich in food and water can be an ideal spot to have young and raise them, and so animals will cover enormous distances in order to breed.

Finding their way
So just how do animals find their way across the planet? Some use visible clues to navigate, such as the positions of the Sun, Moon and even the stars. Others rely on invisible pointers, including Earth's magnetic field, and even their sense of smell!

Changing times
Climate change is altering life for all living things, causing droughts, floods, food shortages and the loss of habitats. Animals are changing their migration routes in search of food and safe places to breed.

LONGEST MIGRATION
ARCTIC TERN
ABOUT 90,000 KM

HIGHEST MIGRATION
BAR-HEADED GOOSE
UP TO 10,175 M

SHORTEST BIRD MIGRATION
BLUE GROUSE
300 M

Wildebeest

CROSSING THE SERENGETI

In May and June each year, the rainy season comes to an end on the grasslands of Africa's Serengeti. Huge herds of wildebeest, zebras and other animals migrate in search of something to drink.

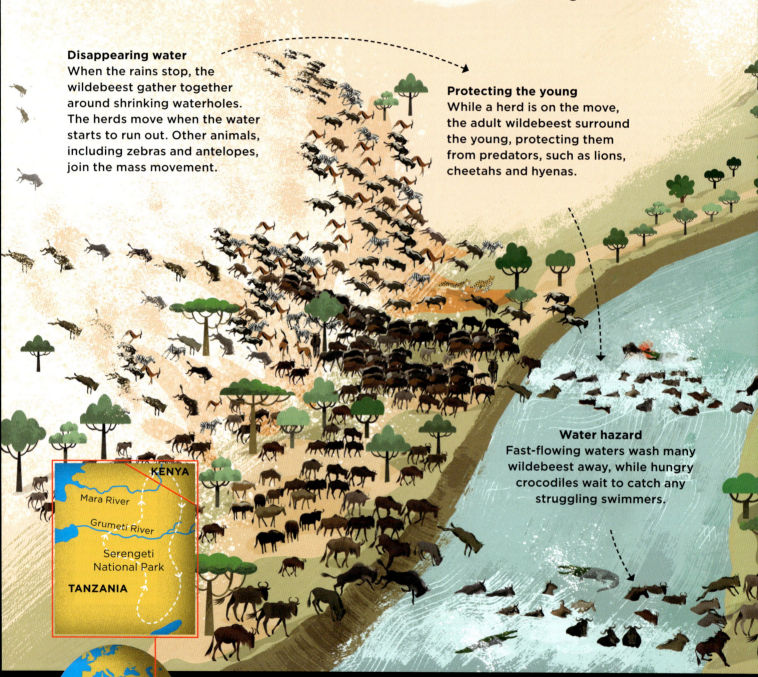

Disappearing water
When the rains stop, the wildebeest gather together around shrinking waterholes. The herds move when the water starts to run out. Other animals, including zebras and antelopes, join the mass movement.

Protecting the young
While a herd is on the move, the adult wildebeest surround the young, protecting them from predators, such as lions, cheetahs and hyenas.

Water hazard
Fast-flowing waters wash many wildebeest away, while hungry crocodiles wait to catch any struggling swimmers.

KENYA
Mara River
Grumeti River
Serengeti National Park
TANZANIA

AFRICA

WILDEBEEST

Number of wildebeest – 1.5 million

Distance travelled – 800 km

Purpose of migration – water, food and a place to give birth

AT THE PEAK OF THE CALVING SEASON,

8,000

WILDEBEEST ARE BORN EACH DAY.

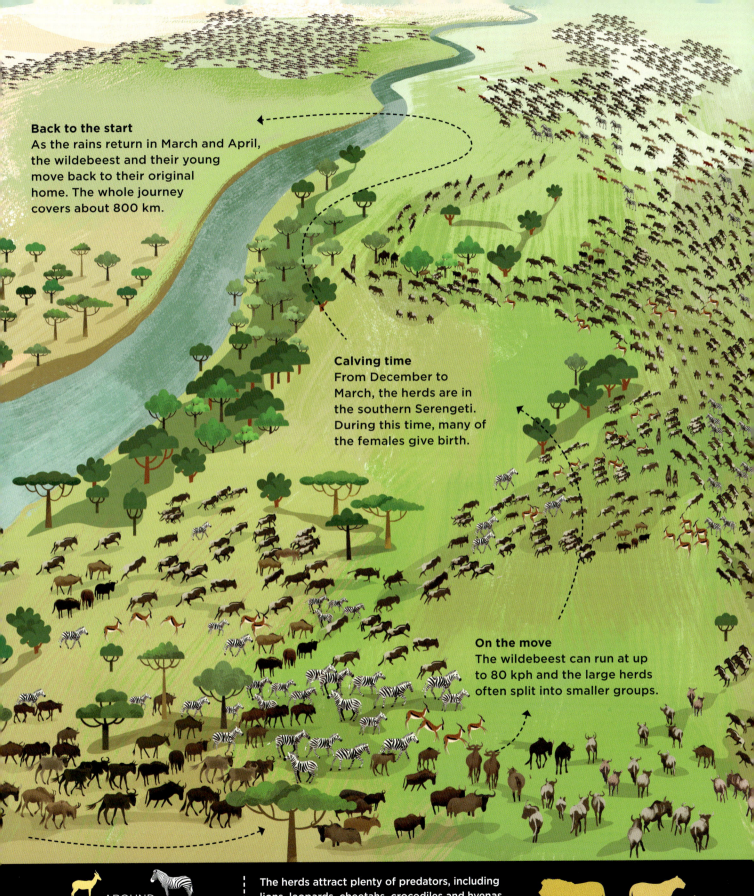

Back to the start
As the rains return in March and April, the wildebeest and their young move back to their original home. The whole journey covers about 800 km.

Calving time
From December to March, the herds are in the southern Serengeti. During this time, many of the females give birth.

On the move
The wildebeest can run at up to 80 kph and the large herds often split into smaller groups.

AROUND
200,000
ZEBRAS AND THOUSANDS OF ANTELOPES

The herds attract plenty of predators, including lions, leopards, cheetahs, crocodiles and hyenas.

Each year, about 250,000 migrating wildebeest and 30,000 zebras are killed by predators, or by thirst, hunger and exhaustion.

Humpback whales

FROM THE POLES TO THE TROPICS

Every year, humpback whales travel to the icy oceans near the north or south poles to feed. As autumn approaches, they must migrate to warmer water to breed, before returning to the poles the following spring.

Feeding time
In the ocean around Alaska, one group of humpback whales spends the summer feeding on krill, plankton and small fish. Food is plentiful in the cold, nutrient-rich water, and the whales eat as much as they can.

Southbound
As winter arrives, the whales head south. They swim non-stop for up to eight weeks, covering about 5,000 km. Their destination is the warmer waters of the tropical Pacific.

Alaska

USA

Pacific Ocean

HUMPBACK WHALES

Number of humpback whales – around 80,000

Distance travelled – up to 25,000 km per year

Purpose of migration – to feed in polar waters and breed in tropical waters

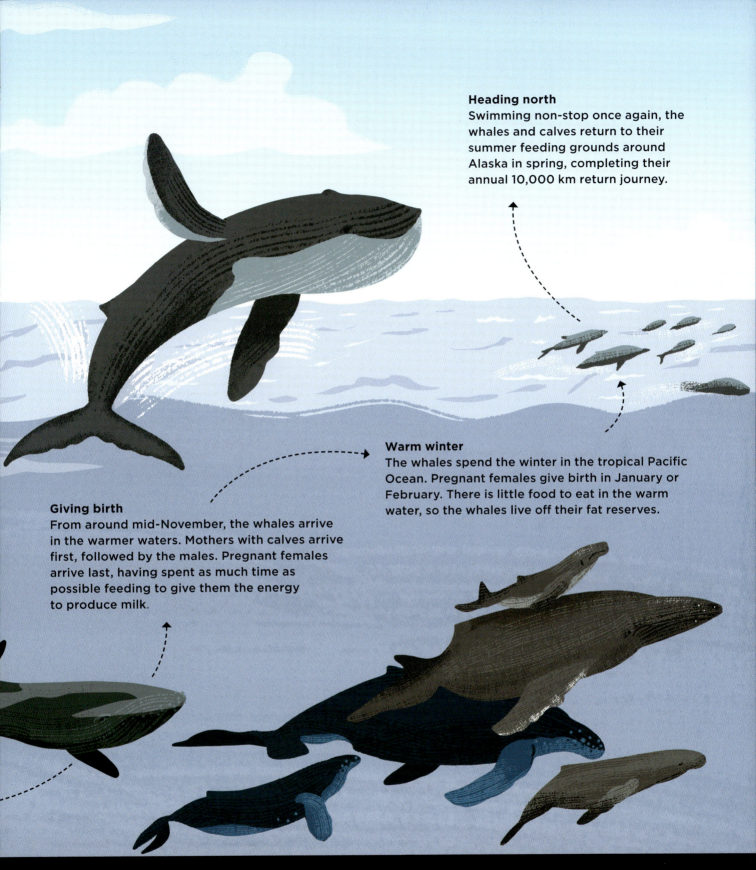

Heading north
Swimming non-stop once again, the whales and calves return to their summer feeding grounds around Alaska in spring, completing their annual 10,000 km return journey.

Warm winter
The whales spend the winter in the tropical Pacific Ocean. Pregnant females give birth in January or February. There is little food to eat in the warm water, so the whales live off their fat reserves.

Giving birth
From around mid-November, the whales arrive in the warmer waters. Mothers with calves arrive first, followed by the males. Pregnant females arrive last, having spent as much time as possible feeding to give them the energy to produce milk.

DURING THE SUMMER, A HUMPBACK WHALE EATS

2.5 TONNES

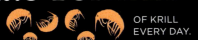

OF KRILL EVERY DAY.

HUMPBACK WHALES ARE THOUGHT TO MAKE THE LONGEST MIGRATIONS OF ANY MAMMAL.

Each group of humpback whales makes a different journey. A small group in the Arabian Sea does not migrate at all.

Monarch butterflies

MEXICO TO CANADA – AND BACK!

Every year, these insects complete a remarkable journey. Over several generations, they travel from Mexico and California to Canada to breed. Then a single generation flies all the way back to avoid the chilly north!

Mexican winter
High in the mountains of central Mexico, millions of monarchs gather on the branches of fir trees. Here, they huddle together to see out the winter.

New generation
In spring, the monarchs fly north to Texas, USA, where they lay eggs on milkweed plants. The eggs hatch into caterpillars.

Long migration
Near the end of summer, the monarchs reach Canada, 5,000 km north of central Mexico. These butterflies are the great-grandchildren of the insects that started the migration six months earlier!

Flying north
After a few weeks, the caterpillars pupate into butterflies. They continue to fly north to find more milkweed and lay more eggs. These eggs produce a new generation that flies further north.

Back south
The monarchs fly south to avoid winter. A single generation crosses the USA to central Mexico, where they will spend the winter before starting the next year's migration.

CANADA
USA
MEXICO

MONARCH BUTTERFLY

Number of monarch butterflies – up to 300 million

Distance travelled each day – 45 km

Purpose of migration – to avoid cold winters and breed

- -

LIFE CYCLE

1. Eggs

2. Caterpillar

3. Pupa

4. Adult

- -

MIGRATION MYSTERY

How do monarch butterflies find their way from Mexico to Canada and back? Scientists think they use a range of clues, such as the Sun, magnetic fields and smell. They may also use natural landmarks to guide them.

Caribou

JOURNEY ACROSS THE TUNDRA

No other land animal travels as far every year as the caribou of Alaska, USA. As spring arrives, huge herds, numbering hundreds of thousands, gather to migrate north to the tundra where they will give birth and raise their young.

Spring start
By the end of March, the caribou are at the northern edge of their winter grazing grounds. The herd then splits. Pregnant females and older caribou leave first, heading north to the coast. They are followed a few weeks later by the bulls (males) and other young caribou.

Crossing rivers
On their way, the caribou have to cross icy rivers. Their thick coats have light, hollow hairs, which keep the caribou warm, and help them to stay afloat.

CARIBOU

Number of caribou – around 950,000
Distance travelled every year – 5,000 km
Purpose of migration – to calve in warmer temperatures

Climate change

With Alaska seeing warmer winters and wetter summers, the caribou's migrations are changing. Warmer weather means the caribou are staying further north for longer periods.

Return to the south

Towards the end of August, the caribou start their migration south again. They eat while moving to build up fat reserves. Males and females mate in the middle of October before the freezing winter months.

Mosquito torture

During June and July, swarms of insects, such as mosquitoes, attack the caribou. To avoid them, the caribou try to stay in windy places or keep moving.

Calving

By the end of May, the caribou have reached the calving grounds where they give birth. Here, warmer temperatures help plants such as sedges and tundra flowers to grow, providing plenty of food for caribou calves.

56 KPH
THE SPEED A CARIBOU CAN RUN AT

CARIBOU ARE KNOWN AS REINDEER IN EUROPE.

CARIBOU CALVES STAND WITHIN AN HOUR OF BEING BORN.

Salmon

SWIMMING THROUGH RIVERS AND OCEANS

During their lives, Pacific salmon go through amazing changes as they migrate thousands of kilometres from rivers and streams in North America out to the Pacific Ocean, before returning to breed in the streams where they hatched.

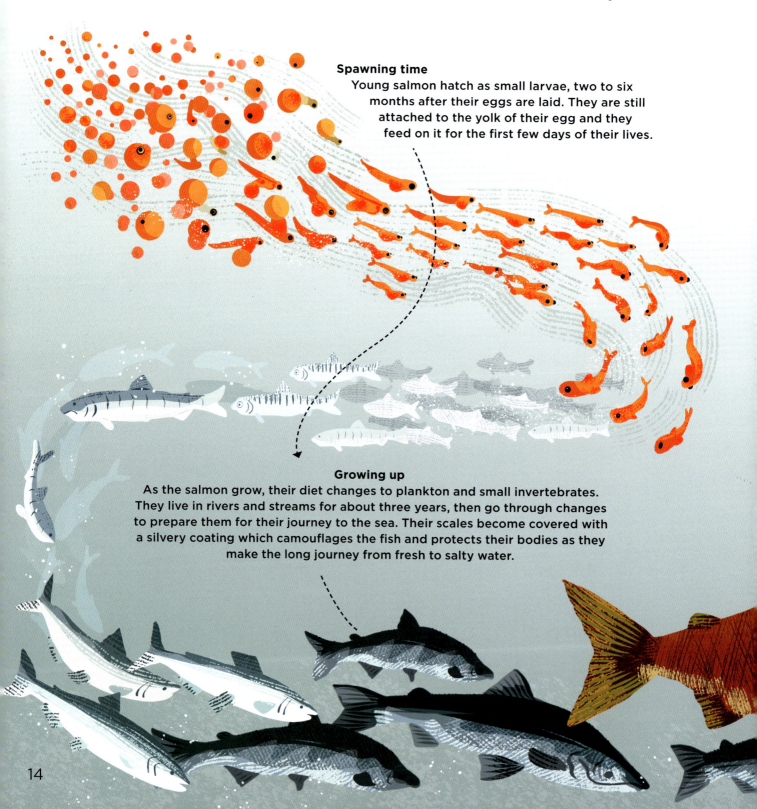

Spawning time
Young salmon hatch as small larvae, two to six months after their eggs are laid. They are still attached to the yolk of their egg and they feed on it for the first few days of their lives.

Growing up
As the salmon grow, their diet changes to plankton and small invertebrates. They live in rivers and streams for about three years, then go through changes to prepare them for their journey to the sea. Their scales become covered with a silvery coating which camouflages the fish and protects their bodies as they make the long journey from fresh to salty water.

The end
Once at the spawning site, female
salmon build a nest called a redd in which
they lay their eggs, each about the size of
a small pea. Once the eggs have been fertilised, the
adult salmon soon die, their life cycle complete.

Heading home
The salmon use their keen sense of smell to find their
way back to the river or stream in which they hatched.
On the way, they have to overcome many obstacles –
including waterfalls – where hungry bears may wait to
catch the salmon as they leap out of the water!

Out to sea
Once out in the Pacific,
the fish spend up to
four years growing
into adult salmon.
When they are ready
to breed, they return
to the waterway in which
they hatched, where their
bodies go through more
changes. They grow darker
in colour. Males grow large
humps on their backs, sharp teeth
and a hook or curve on the ends of
their jaws in order to attract a mate.

NORTH
AMERICA
Pacific
Ocean

SALMON

**Size of a Chinook
salmon –** up to 1.5 m
long and 60 kg in weight

Distance travelled –
16,000 km

**Purpose of migration
–** to feed and grow into
an adult

- - - - - - - - - - - - - - -

5,000
THE NUMBER OF EGGS
EACH FEMALE SALMON
LAYS IN ITS REDD.

- - - - - - - - - - - - - - -

**SCIENTISTS BELIEVE
THAT SALMON CAN
DETECT EARTH'S
MAGNETIC FIELD
AND USE IT TO FIND
THE OPENING TO
THEIR HATCH RIVER.**

- - - - - - - - - - - - - - -

SALMON HAVE BEEN
SEEN JUMPING
VERTICALLY ALMOST

4 M

Arctic terns
LONGEST ANIMAL MIGRATION

With a migration route from the Arctic to Antarctica and back again, these birds cover up to 90,000 km every year on their hunt for food – more than twice around the planet and further than any other animal.

Breeding time

Arctic terns arrive at their northern breeding grounds in May and early June. The females lay between one and three eggs in a nest scraped into the ground. After they hatch, the adults feed their young on small fish and sea invertebrates. The young terns are ready to fly when they are a few weeks old.

Heading south

By the end of July, the birds are ready to fly south. The trip can take several months and many terns will wander far from the usual route. One tern from the UK was discovered 22,000 km away in Australia!

ARCTIC
AFRICA
SOUTH AMERICA
ANTARCTICA

ARCTIC TERN
Number of arctic tern – around 1,000,000
Total distance travelled – 90,000 km
Purpose of migration – to feed and find warmer weather

30 The average age an Arctic tern can reach

Back north again

As the southern summer comes to a close, the birds find their way back to the Arctic along the same routes they followed south. Incredibly, the birds always return to the same breeding grounds, even after a journey of tens of thousands of kilometres.

Down to Antarctica

On the way south, terns usually follow the coasts of the major continents. They then spread out over the Southern Ocean where they feed. To eat, they dip down to the water's surface to snatch up small fish.

BY TRAVELLING FROM THE ARCTIC SUMMER TO THE ANTARCTIC SUMMER, ARCTIC TERNS SEE MORE DAYLIGHT PER YEAR THAN ANY OTHER ANIMAL.

OVER ITS LIFETIME, AN ARCTIC TERN CAN FLY UP TO

2,500,000 KM.

THAT'S THE SAME AS FLYING TO THE MOON AND BACK THREE TIMES.

European eels

MYSTERY MIGRATION

Every year, adult eels leave rivers across Europe for the Atlantic Ocean, heading to their spawning grounds in the Sargasso Sea. Small juvenile eels eventually swim back the other way, but very little is known about what happens to the eels on their journey.

Ocean hatching
Hatching in the Sargasso Sea, the young eels emerge as tiny, see-through larvae. These young eels are still attached to the egg yolk and get all the nutrients they need from this.

Riding the ocean currents
The larvae drift on ocean currents towards Europe. During this time, they grow to around 10 cm long. Just before they reach the Atlantic coast, they enter the next stage of their development and are known as glass eels.

River run
As they enter a river, the eels carry on growing. They turn yellow-brown and are now known as yellow eels. They spend up to 20 years in the river, feeding on small fish, molluscs and crustaceans and growing up to 1.5 m long.

EUROPEAN EEL

Life expectancy – up to 20 years
Distance travelled to spawning site – 8,000 km
Purpose of migration – to feed and spawn

Scientists believe that eels can detect Earth's magnetic field and use it to find their way, like an internal compass.

Mystery migration
As they leave the rivers, the eels' intestines dissolve and they can no longer feed. Very little is known about this migration back to the Sargasso Sea, where the eels spawn and lay eggs before dying.

Return to the sea
When the eels are ready to breed, their bodies change again. They turn silver and their eyes get bigger to prepare them for their migration to the murkier ocean. Now known as silver eels, they swim back into the ocean and start their migration back towards the Sargasso Sea.

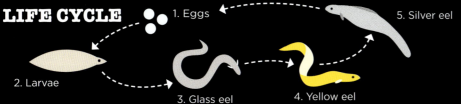

LIFE CYCLE
1. Eggs
2. Larvae
3. Glass eel
4. Yellow eel
5. Silver eel

NO SILVER EELS HAVE EVER BEEN CAUGHT IN THE OPEN OCEAN ON THEIR WAY TO THE SPAWNING GROUNDS.

Globe skimmer dragonflies

INCREDIBLE INSECT ODYSSEY

Globe skimmer dragonflies make an amazing journey that lasts several generations and covers thousands of kilometres. Their journey across the Indian Ocean is one of the most amazing global migrations.

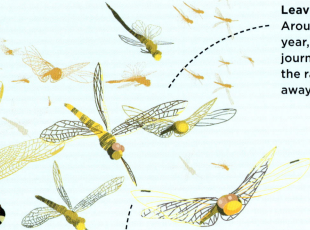

Leaving the dry season
Around August and September each year, millions of dragonflies start their journey southwest from India in search of the rainy season thousands of kilometres away in eastern Africa.

Crossing the ocean
As they set off across the Indian Ocean, the insects are joined by birds, such as falcons and nightjars. They fly on the same winds as the dragonflies, eating some of the insects on their way.

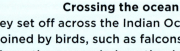

An island stop
The dragonflies find their way to one of the thousands of small islands dotted across the Indian Ocean. Here, the dragonflies mate and lay eggs in small pools of rainwater before dying. After hatching, the new dragonflies continue the mass migration to Africa.

Homeward bound
As the rains dry up in Africa, the dragonflies start their long journey back across the Indian Ocean. They stop off again on islands to feed, rest and breed, before arriving back in India in time for the next rainy season.

Reaching Africa
Another journey across hundreds of kilometres of ocean brings the dragonflies to the coasts of southern Africa. Here, they lay more eggs and feed during the rainy season.

GLOBE SKIMMER DRAGONFLY

Distance flown by single dragonfly – up to 6,000 km

Total distance of round trip – 18,000 km

Purpose of migration – to find water, feed and breed

6,300 M

THE HEIGHT GLOBE SKIMMERS HAVE BEEN RECORDED AT, MAKING THEM THE HIGHEST-FLYING DRAGONFLY SPECIES.

WITH A STRONG TAILWIND, A DRAGONFLY CAN FLY THE 800 KM FROM INDIA TO THE MALDIVES IN JUST 24 HOURS.

Plankton

EVERYDAY VERTICAL MIGRATION

Every day in lakes and oceans around the world, billions of microscopic animals move up from the deep to feed near the surface. This journey may be short, but the huge numbers of creatures taking part make it one of the biggest migrations on the planet.

Tiny hunters

These migrating creatures are zooplankton – a collection of tiny creatures, such as krill, as well as the young of larger sea creatures, such as eels and squid.

Sun bathing

Just like land plants, phytoplankton capture the Sun's energy and use it to convert carbon dioxide and water into sugars and oxygen – a process called photosynthesis. They have to live close to the surface because very little sunlight can reach below 200 m.

Sunset safari

As the Sun sets, the zooplankton rise up to the water's surface. They are looking for their favourite food – tiny plants called phytoplankton. These tasty snacks live in the upper layer of the water, where daytime hunting would be too dangerous for the zooplankton as they could become prey themselves.

Back down again
Throughout the night,
the zooplankton catch and
eat phytoplankton. Then, as
the Sun rises, the zooplankton
sink back down to the dark
depths of the water.

Solar eclipses
have been
known to lure
zooplankton
up from the
water's depths.

THE
ZOOPLANKTON'S
MOVEMENT
PATTERN IS CALLED
DIEL (DAILY)
VERTICAL
MIGRATION (DVM).

ZOOPLANKTON

Number of zooplankton – billions
Zooplankton habitat – the deep sea (below 200 m)
Purpose of migration – to feed at the ocean surface

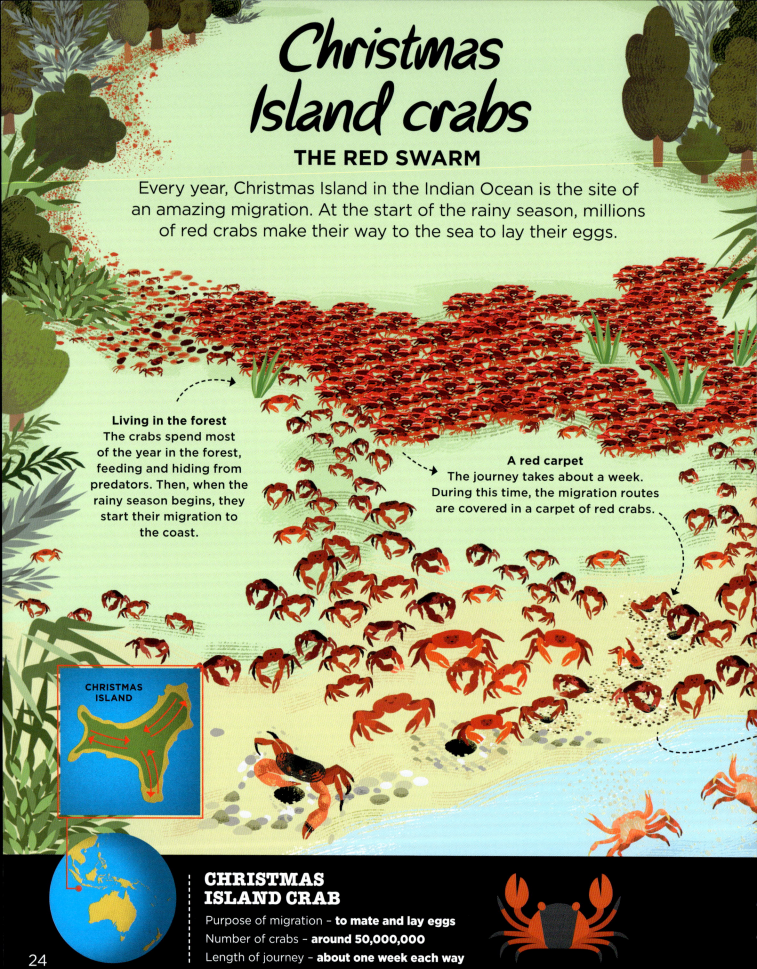

Christmas Island crabs

THE RED SWARM

Every year, Christmas Island in the Indian Ocean is the site of an amazing migration. At the start of the rainy season, millions of red crabs make their way to the sea to lay their eggs.

Living in the forest
The crabs spend most of the year in the forest, feeding and hiding from predators. Then, when the rainy season begins, they start their migration to the coast.

A red carpet
The journey takes about a week. During this time, the migration routes are covered in a carpet of red crabs.

CHRISTMAS ISLAND

CHRISTMAS ISLAND CRAB

Purpose of migration – **to mate and lay eggs**
Number of crabs – **around 50,000,000**
Length of journey – **about one week each way**

Return to the forest
The young crabs emerge from the sea and start their march back to the forest. They spend another four to five years maturing before they migrate back to the water to have young of their own.

Laying eggs
When they reach the beach, male crabs dig a burrow where they mate with females before returning to the forest. Around two weeks later, the females go down to the sea to release their eggs into the water.

Growing young
The young crabs hatch as soon as the eggs are laid, and they stay in the water for three to four weeks. During this time, they attract predators, such as manta rays and whale sharks.

ISLANDERS HAVE BUILT 'CRAB GRIDS' – SPECIAL UNDERPASSES THAT GO UNDER ROADS – AND EVEN 5-M-HIGH BRIDGES SO THAT THE CRABS CAN CROSS ROADS SAFELY.

The introduction of the yellow crazy ant from Australia led to a 30 per cent reduction in the red crab population. Tiny wasps were later introduced in an effort to control the ant population.

Army ants

MIGRATION OF DESTRUCTION

Swarming across the forest floor, millions of army ants carve a path of destruction to keep their colony alive. These terrifying insects raid one area before moving to another. Don't get in their way!

Ant colony
An army ant colony can contain more than 15 million ants. These are divided into blind worker ants, soldier ants with large, powerful jaws, large males and a single queen, whose job it is to mate with the males and lay eggs.

On the move
About ten days after the queen has laid her eggs, the colony migrates in search of food, moving along in a column before forming a temporary home, called a bivouac.

USA

SOUTH AMERICA

ARMY ANTS

Number of ants in a colony – over 15 million
Number of eggs an army ant queen can lay – 4,000,000
Purpose of migration – to feed the colony

A COLONY OF ARMY ANTS CAN EAT ALMOST 100,000 PREY ANIMALS EVERY SINGLE DAY.

Taking advantage
Waiting in the trees nearby are birds who snatch up any fleeing prey animals. Once they have exhausted the local food supply, army ants will migrate to another area.

Hunting parties
Columns of workers go out to forage for food. These columns can be 20 m wide and more than 100 m long! In a single hour, an army ant raid can carry off 3,000 prey animals, from other insects to small birds and mammals.

Living camp
The bivouac is formed from millions of ants. They lock their jaws, legs and other body parts together to make a living structure. Inside are chambers for the food, larvae and eggs, and the queen. Soldier ants stand by, ready to defend the bivouac with their powerful jaws.

A QUEEN ARMY ANT CAN LIVE FOR

10–20
YEARS.

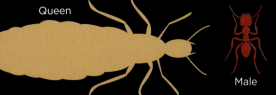

Queen

Male

As well as bivouacs, army ants build other structures using their bodies, including tunnels and even bridges to cross obstacles.

27

Emperor penguins

MARCH THROUGH THE ICY WORLD

While most animals migrate to warmer regions during the winter, emperor penguins march into the frozen Antarctic to raise their young. But as climate change sees sea ice melting, we are losing the habitat that emperor penguins rely on.

Feeding time
From January to March, the adult penguins feed and mate in the Antarctic waters, which are rich in nutrients and fish during these warmer summer months.

The long march
At the end of March, the adults migrate about 150 km inland to their nesting grounds. Here, the females lay one egg each and pass them on to the males who store their eggs in incubating pouches to keep them warm.

Atlantic Ocean

ANTARCTICA

Southern Ocean

EMPEROR PENGUINS

Number of emperor penguins – over 590,000

Distance travelled – about 160 km each way

Purpose of migration – to raise their young

During the winter months, Antarctic temperatures can drop to

-60°C

To the sea
By December, the chicks have grown and replaced their downy feathers with waterproof ones. The parents and young then march back to the Southern Ocean to feed in the sea.

The return
The eggs start to hatch in August and the females return. Among the huge crowds, they locate their mate and their young by their calls. The males now leave to feed, while the females feed the chicks on pieces of fish they bring up from their stomachs.

Long cold winter
The female emperor penguins then migrate back across the ice, walking and sliding their way to the sea to feed. As temperatures plummet, the males huddle together in their thousands to keep themselves – and their eggs – warm.

By the end of the winter, male penguins can lose up to 40 per cent of their body weight.

EMPEROR PENGUINS ARE THE LARGEST PENGUIN SPECIES, STANDING ABOUT 1.2 M TALL.

THEY CAN DIVE TO DEPTHS OF MORE THAN 500 M AND STAY UNDERWATER FOR MORE THAN 20 MINUTES.

Glossary

Bivouac the name given to a temporary camp

Bull the name given to the males of some species, such as elephants and whales

Camouflage a pattern or colouring that allows plants and animals to blend in with their environment

Climate change long-term changes to average weather conditions

Crustacean animal with a hard outer shell and several pairs of jointed legs

Fertilise when the egg from a female animal joins with the sperm from a male animal

Fry young, very small fish

Generation a group of living things that are born around the same time

Herd a large group of animals

Invertebrate an animal that doesn't have a spine

Juvenile a young animal

Larvae an early stage in the life cycle of some animals, just after it has hatched from an egg

Magnetic field the invisible force around a magnet that attracts or repels other magnetic materials

Mammal type of animal that usually gives birth to live young and produces milk to feed to their young

Migration the movement of animals from one place to another in search of food, water or somewhere to raise young

FURTHER INFORMATION

WEBSITES
www.natgeokids.com
www.nasa.gov/kidsclub
www.oceanservice.noaa.gov/kids/

MUSEUMS
Science Museum
Exhibition Road, South Kensington, London SW7 2DD

Oxford University Museum of Natural History
Parks Rd, Oxford, OX1 3PW

Navigate to find the right direction in which to travel

Nutrients nourishing foods or substances that enable living things to function and grow

Photosynthesis the process by which plants use sunlight to convert carbon dioxide and water into sugar and oxygen

Phytoplankton tiny living things that live in water and use photosynthesis to produce the food they need to survive

Poles the regions around the very top and bottom of Earth

Predator an animal that hunts and kills other animals for food

Pupate when the larva of an animal changes into a pupa, just before it matures into its adult form

Solar eclipse when the Moon passes in front of the Sun and casts a shadow on Earth

Spawning producing eggs

Tailwind a wind that blows from behind, helping to push a vehicle or animal along

Tropics the regions of Earth that lie either side of the Equator

Tundra used to describe a cold region where the soil is frozen all year round and where no trees grow

Waterhole a natural pool of water

Zooplankton tiny animals that live in water

BOOKS

Ecographics: Biodiversity by Izzi Howell (Franklin Watts, 2019).
Discover the environmental challenges affecting animals and ecosystems with graphics, facts and case studies.

Mapographica: The Natural World by Jon Richards and Ed Simkins (Wayland, 2015).
Explore the world's biodiversity hotspots and longest animal migrations with innovative infographics and absorbing facts.

Index